THE POWER OF POSITIVE ~RECOGNITION~

By

Ronald K. Claiborne

authorHOUSE™

1663 Liberty Drive, Suite 200
Bloomington, Indiana 47403
(800) 839-8640
www.AuthorHouse.com

AuthorHouse™
1663 Liberty Drive, Suite 200
Bloomington, IN 47403
www.authorhouse.com
Phone: 1-800-839-8640

AuthorHouse™ *UK Ltd.*
500 Avebury Boulevard
Central Milton Keynes, MK9 2BE
www.authorhouse.co.uk
Phone: 08001974150

First published by AuthorHouse 2/15/2006

ISBN: 1-4259-0460-2 (sc)

*Printed in the United States of America
Bloomington, Indiana*

This book is printed on acid-free paper.

AKNOWLEDGEMENTS

To a loving family who did not question

The passion I had for writing and who

Endured times when I seemed far off in a

world all to myself. They have inspired me to

reach for the stars. Thank you for being there

when I needed you most.

Thanks to my advisor whom I bounced

Many ideas off and who suffered through

Many bad drafts of this project and gave me

Honest criticism for my work.

God Bless Each of You.

CONTENTS

CHAPTER 1

Why Positive Recognition?

"The computer can return information based only on the information it is given by the programmer. If the programmer does his work well, the information received will be worthwhile and useful; if he fails to write the program correctly, the information produced will be negative and useless. The human mind is no different! Your mind is the computer and you are the computer programmer. If you put positive information in, the results will be positive and worthwhile. If you feed your mind-computer negative information, the results will be negative and directed toward failure". Bland p. 32.

Positive recognition, "the act of recognizing or the acknowledgement of a fact or claim", therefore is critical to the development of a successful life in all of its aspects. Preble p.1054. Catching somebody doing the right thing, even catching yourself, and then giving positive reinforcement truly help build self esteem. The use of positive reinforcement or recognition then can be a powerful force in molding and shaping our lives. This power, once it is learned, can be applied to oneself or to others with the same beneficial results. "A successful life" according to Ari Kiev in A Strategy for Daily Living, "does not result from chance nor is it determined by fate or good fortune, but from a succession of successful days". Therefore it becomes important that individuals who are striving to have a successful life learn to set goals and make strategic action plans. When dealing with people who are just learning to do this it is important they program their minds for success instead of failure. Positive recognition helps to build an environment that supports success instead of failure. To build positive self esteem, to change the direction of ones life, to achieve excellence all require the same dedication to achieving the goals that have been set. Just about all of us make New Year's Resolution's but few of us actually see them accomplished. All this can be changed through positive recognition. Anthony Robbins in Unlimited Power p. 69 wrote, "the path of success consists of knowing your outcome, taking action, knowing what results you're getting, and having the flexibility to change until you are successful". To the person new to establishing a success system for their life it is important they experience a succession of small successes supported by positive recognition or positive reinforcement. This can be accomplished by responding positively to all successes very quickly after the deed has been

3

accomplished. Dr. Robert Sharpe and David Lewis say in their book The Success Factor "it is the speed rather than the lavish distant reward that makes the difference. The more immediate a piece of behavior is followed by a reinforcer the more effective the reinforcer will be in establishing that behavior".

CHAPTER 2

How Can We Help Our Children?

"Children could learn from a properly reactive environment and limits in their conduct could be attributed to limitations in the ability to construct an environment rather than limitations within the children, their genetic history, or their environmental background. Once again the successes with which laboratory procedures were able to control and influence behavior reinforced the belief that even the most difficult human problems could be solved by a deliberate and rational application of a proper environment". Ferster p. 5. Teaching children to set goals, to develop personal mission statements, and to write their values is not enough. Young people need to learn these techniques as they are going through the process of living each day. Therefore, allowing children to learn while they are in a relaxed but stimulated state of mind helps them to make sense out of the information being filtered into their brains. In doing this the nervous system is made an ally to the learning process. What needs to be done is to "make automatic and habitual, as early as possible, as many useful actions as we can, and guard against the growing into ways that are likely to be disadvantageous to us, as we should against the plagues. The more of the details of our daily life we can hand over to the effortless custody of automation, the more our higher power of mind will be set free for their own proper work". James p. 131. We can help children best by helping them set goals and then helping them to successfully achieve each goal in the course of activity. We must remember our decisions will ultimately determine the quality of life. This should encourage all of us to take time to learn and teach the art of making right decisions right. Children will struggle more in this area because they do not have the historical data stored away in memory to aide the decision making process. Some adults struggle because the decision making process is based upon faulty information stored in memory and the bank of bad habits that have been reinforced over time. To help those who are at risk we either need to interrupt the old way of doing things or prevent the development of bad habits. If we would only take the time to practice doing even the littlest things right everyday we will over a period of time develop the right habits that will grow into the right behavior. Many of us are unaware we create an environment that contributes to the development of our lives as well as the lives of our children. I like to believe we are the product of our environment. In fact, "the environment of a subject to be changed must first be stabilized before attempting to condition a new behavior response". Ferster p. 13. It makes a difference when we write down our goals and then develop a step by step action plan of how we will achieve our goals. It makes a difference if we understand what makes us do what we do. It is good to know I get angry when someone makes remarks about my family because I value my family very highly. Knowing this, I can now get better control over myself because I now know why I am angry and can now make a decision to change for the better. The ability to be successful in reaching my goals is greatly enhanced if I can work in a stable environment. Knowing what need to be done is one thing but getting ourselves to do it is another.

CHAPTER 3

How to Get Ourselves on Our Side

Children as well as adults need help in navigating the rough waters of life. From the cradle to the grave we are faced with challenges that sometimes threaten to derail all our efforts. It seems the harder we try to make things better the worse they seem to get. There is a solution to this dilemma. There is a way we can get ourselves on our side. There are tools and systems that can help us as they have helped many other people. I have discovered after reading many books on the subject of success that the same information is repeated over and over again. Even I am not writing anything new in these pages. What I am doing is helping each of us to realize who is really standing in the way of our success. Have you ever given thought to whom has made decisions for you all your life? It comes as a great surprise to many they have made their own decisions since the day they were born. When you were wet you made a decision to get dry and you acted upon that decision by crying and you cried until you were attended too. When you were hungry you cried as a baby until you were fed. This is a continuous list knowing what you want, making a decision to do something about it, analyzing the results of your actions, and remaining flexible to try a new strategy if the first one failed. We use to naturally do what many are now writing books or doing seminars to teach us to do. What happened? We got use to the safety net. Many of us had loving parents who served as our safety nets when we made our earlier decisions and therefore if our parents did not remove the net soon enough we grew comfortable with making safe decisions. We then gradually turned over the decision making process to others in our lives in an effort to maintain the safety net. We stopped being risk takers. We stopped exploring our world and we became complacent with status quo. To change that stinking thinking we must deliberately and consciously make a decision to reclaim control over our lives. Having a positive mental attitude helps but it alone cannot change a life time of bad habits and bad decision making. You need a plan. You need a strategy of how you will begin to rebuild your life. It is important to note right here that if you are not willing to make the decision to change and make a commitment to change, it will not happen for you. Every program works. It is you that do not work. To change you have to want it deep down inside your heart. To change you will need to know in your heart a failure to change at this precise moment in time will mean total destruction of your life as you know it. Until you get to the point of no return, until you get to the point it will hurt you more to stay as you

11

are then it will for you to change you will not commit to the decision you have made. You would have been just practicing wishful thinking and hoping by chance it will happen the way you dreamed it would. The power of positive recognition will help you to face the facts and make the necessary changes one step at a time so you can experience success at establishing and reaching your goals little by little. It is important to note here that goals must require you to stretch beyond your comfort zone in order for you to derive a benefit from the goal. Therefore I advocate setting short term goals that are well within your capability to reach, intermediate goals that will require you to be just a little uncomfortable, and long term goals that are realistic but beyond your present reach. Goals should be attainable, goals should be specific, and goals should be in line with your value structure or you will not give the attaining of them your full attention.

Getting ourselves on our side begins with the recognition we are somebody. We all have been made in the image of God and when he made us he says it is good. It is important we recognize the importance of our being born so let us start with our purpose here on earth. It is important each of us take time to do three things before we begin to develop our strategic plan for our lives. We need to write a personal mission statement, we need to write down our goals, and we need to write down our values. A mission statement will help us see what is important in our life. It focuses on "what we want to be (character) and to do (contributions and achievements) and on the values or principles upon being and doing are based. Covey p. 106. By focusing on your personal mission statement you will be able to stay focused on what you are trying to accomplish in life. This will help you when you are writing goals and developing New Year Resolutions. A mission statement reminds you of who you are and what is important to you in life. Our goals outline what it is we wish to accomplish in life. Goals that are specific tell us when we want to accomplish them and goals should be realistic so we will believe in them. Values are those things we hold that are of the greatest importance to us. Things such as love, truth, honesty, God, and family are examples of values. Values are the principles by which we live our lives. It is important here to mention that these three areas are always consulted by our sub conscious mind before we make any decisions. When you can master these areas along with writing a personal strategic plan that has action steps then you are well on your way to success. When you make a decision to change something in your life for the better you should take time to recognize that moment in some way. You can reward your self by giving yourself a treat or let someone else know how proud you are of the big step you have made and you will see the power of positive recognition begin working inside of you.

CHAPTER 4

How to Write Your Own Personal Mission Statement

As child I use to sit down with my brothers and we use to dream about what we would be when we grew up. One said he was going into the army, another said he would be a star in the NFL, and I had no earthly idea what I wanted to do or be in life. When I look back on that time I realize now I could have benefited from a structured approach to life. It would have been nice if I had a personal success coach who could have guided me into the right path. Instead when I was a senior in high school I went to the school's library to select a career. I selected a library book on careers and picked Accounting as my course of study. I went to college and majored in accounting and graduated with honors only to discover this was not what I wanted to do with my life. I could have used a vocational counselor back then to help me define and then achieve my goals in life. It would have been the vocational counselor's role to help me:

> "1. Become better acquainted with myself and recognize and accept my assets and liabilities
>
> 2. Become acquainted with the world of work, its range, nature, demands, and opportunities
>
> 3. Become acquainted with my development and to become acquainted with my role in the world of work and the objectives that I sought to achieve
>
> 4. Become motivated to achieve my objectives".
>
> Dudycha P. 102

All of this could have been accomplished by following some advice given by Stephen C Covey in his book The 7 Habits of Highly Effective People "to begin with the end in mind". "To begin with the end in mind," he continues means" to start with a clear understanding of your destination. It means to know where you're going so that you better understand where you are now and so the steps you take are always in the right direction". Covey p. 98. A mission statement then is your personal blueprint for success in life. With it you will discover life takes on purpose and meaning. When a personal mission statement is read about you it should reflect who you are in your heart. A personal mission statement should be general and not overly specific. Being too specific here will leave little room for flexibility and may cause you to feel you have not achieved your purpose. Remember you want to bring positive recognition to each phase of your life. Therefore when you write your mission statement it should be stated in positive terms and should talk about what you want to be and do as an individual. It may be easier to do an analysis of yourself before starting the mission statement. You can begin by writing a short essay on whom you are and make sure in this process you include the things that are important in your life-your values.

The self analysis should cover an inventory of your strengths, weaknesses, opportunities, and threats. This will help you see what you are good at doing and what you need to avoid. When writing the mission statement start with a general statement of what you want your life to accomplish then venture into what type of person you would have to be and what things you would have to do and learn to achieve this goal.

CHAPTER 5

Setting Positive Recognition Goals

Goal setting for those who have never taken the time to do it can be a very challenging event in their life. We grow as individuals when we see our dreams come to reality. Our lives are rich and full because of the energy we get from accomplishing something worthwhile. If you are like me and many others in this world sometimes we have a hard time moving from the dream state to the state of reality. Many of the dreams I had as a child have remained just a dream. It has often amazed me how some people can accomplish so much with so little. The power of positive recognition when applied to goal setting can help both you and I to overcome our handicaps. You might recall we said earlier that" recognition is the acknowledgement of a fact or claim which leads us to the conclusion that we can choose to acknowledge the positive facts and claims or the negative facts and claims. The question is how do we go from being a non-achiever to one who is capable of accomplishing just about everything we can conceive in our mind? Setting positive recognition goals can be beneficial to helping us fulfill our dreams if we will take the time to write down each and every goal we have. One of the best things we can do in the beginning is to sit down and write out on paper all of our aspirations or dreams we would like to accomplish in our lives. The aim of positive recognition goal setting is to establish a means to progressively approach each goal in an orderly and systematic manner. According to William James, who wrote The Principles of Psychology, "if an individual keeps faithfully busy each hour of the working day, he may safely leave the final result to itself. He can with perfect certainty count on waking up some fine morning to find himself one of the competent ones of his generation, in whatever pursuit he may have singled out". James p. 131. Because we have the ability to program our minds and have the ability through the concentration of thought and effort to focus on a single cause consistently and persistently, we can accomplish any goal we decide is worthy of our attention. Many people are able to take adversity and turn it into success because they possess this trait naturally within.

When setting goals it is important to do the following:

(a) Write down the main goal

(b) Write out the objective of the goal

(c) Write the sub-objectives

(d) Write out when you expect to achieve the goal

The main goal tells what it is you want to do.

Then the Objective answers the question why you want to do it and sub-objectives allow you to write out where you want to focus your attention. In our chapter on strategic action plans we will address the question how we will implement each step so we can receive positive results. The frequency you use to review your goals is entirely up to you but I find a daily routine of reviewing goals is the most beneficial. One of the main things to do when writing goals is to include a date you expect to reach the goal. This will give the individual a sense of purpose and accomplishment when the milestone is achieved. What must be learned here is that it will take discipline to accomplish any goal set- be them great or small. Even reading this book should help you realize you need to give yourself some positive recognition. In positive recognition goal setting it is important to reinforce each successful step you take toward achieving your goal. When setting goals we must realize we are seeking to acquire new habits.

"In the acquisition of a new habit, or leaving off of an old one, we must take care to launch ourselves with as strong and decided an initiative as possible. Accumulate all the possible circumstances which shall reinforce the right motives; put yourself assiduously in conditions that encourage the new way (goal); make engagements incompatible with the old; take a public pledge, if the case allows; in short, envelop your resolution with every aid you know. This will give your new beginning (goal) such momentum that the temptation to break down will not occur as soon as it otherwise might, and every day during which a breakdown is postponed adds to the chances of it not occurring at all. Never suffer an exception to occur till the new habit (goal) is securely rooted in your life. Continuity of training (or of goal setting and application) is the great means of making the nervous system act infallibly right". Therefore, "the need for securing success at the outset is imperative. Failure at first is apt to dampen the energy of all future attempts, whereas past experiences of success nerves one to future vigor". James p. 131.

CHAPTER 6

Why Values Count

In the course of teaching others to develop a mission statement, write their goals, and write their values I have found many people are fuzzy when thinking about values. Values are what make us tick. According to the New Lexicon Webster's Dictionary of the English language on page 476 Value is defined as "a principle, quality etc. that arouses such desire" that it is "expressed in terms of the effort, money etc. one is willing to expend in acquiring, retaining possession of, or preserving it". Values, as I describe them to my students, are the things that will arouse strong emotions in us. Values when violated often times make us want to fight. It is when we understand our values-those things which are most important to us do we begin to understand ourselves and what causes us to act the way we do. Understanding values is important to any goal setting process because it helps us to understand why we don't accomplish some of our goals. If you have strong values regarding family then it will be very hard for you to set a goal that goes against the very essence of what a family stands for. Subconsciously your mind and inner being will not allow you to violate that which you have programmed your self to believe and hold dear to your heart.   This will require extensive reprogramming of your nervous system to get your body to do what it is being asked to do. Can it be done? Yes it can be done but it will not be very easy to accomplish. This is why positive recognition or reinforcement is important. To accomplish something anything it will require you to focus all your attention and effort in the direction of the thing you want to accomplish. If consciously you desire something but unconsciously you don't it will not occur. There have been times in my life I wanted to lose weight but I failed to get myself on my side. Consciously I wanted to lose weight but none of the actions I took supported what I desired to do. When trying to teach someone about values who have not thought about what is really important to them is challenging. Most of us do not think about what makes us do and say the things we do. In this book on positive recognition the premise is that change can occur when we accentuate the positive steps we make toward achieving our goals. Understanding our values is important because "ways of behavior cannot be reliably produced until they are mastered much as a skill is mastered. To reproduce behavior we must be able to model or produce convincingly bodily, vocal, and emotional ways of behaving. Behavior has two components-what is done and the way in which it is done. Everything done must be done in the same way. Behavior has come to mean what an organism does and habit to mean what an organism does repeatedly". Costall p.35. If we are to change and begin to accomplish our goals we must first begin to understand who we are. This, to me, is one of the most eye opening exercises an individual can do when embarking on a success program and that is to write an essay on who they perceive themselves to be. It must be clearly understood that there are two basic responses we make in every situation, we either stand, and fight or we run away. As individuals we must strive to determine which one of these responses is our natural inclination. Once we learn this we will have uncovered the root cause of the decision path we have chosen to take and can now become empowered to make changes which will give us more control over the direction our lives take. Values are indeed important in the grand scheme of positive recognition.

CHAPTER 7

Developing Your Own Personal Strategic Action Plan

In the preceding pages writing a mission statement, developing goals, and knowing our values have been our main focus but none of this will be of any good if we do not achieve the desired results of accomplishing our goals. Many of us go through life wondering why some people are so lucky. We often ask ourselves why is it those people are always getting the breaks. Others always seem to get the promotions, the better jobs, the best car, and the list goes on and on. Why is it I never seem to get anything I want? The answer to these questions are not simple because there are as many reasons as there are people but there are some things we can do that is common to just about everyone who achieve any level of success. We have spent considerable time in this book talking about some of the tools that need to be used to achieve success but there is still one more ingredient necessary for success. We need a strategic action plan to provide a systematic and orderly way to accomplish our goals. Earlier in this book we listed the formula for success as stated by Anthony Robbins in his book Unlimited Power as "knowing your outcome, taking action, knowing what results you're getting, and having the flexibility to change until you're successful," to illustrate the fact there is no such thing as luck but what we get are the results of the actions we take. Therefore it is important we have a plan in place to accomplish all these wonderful goals we set up. One of the important things we must remember here is that a strategic action plan needs to be designed for each individual. The goal of the strategic action plan is to develop specific strategies or steps that need to be taken in order to achieve the desired results. Each step or strategy of the action plan will be monitored and measured to determine if the desired result is being achieved. Herein lay the problem with this method. Many people want to get a quick fix. They want to get results without going through the process. To be effective a strategic action plan for positive recognition will incorporate rewards with the achievement of each step. A personal strategic action plan can be designed by first writing the mission statement followed by the values statement then the goals in five areas. Goals should be written to cover your spiritual, education, finance, health, and recreation needs. After the mission statement, values statement, and goals have been written each goal need to be further broken down into objectives which will be further boiled down to action steps complete with time frames in which each step, objective, and goal will be achieved. To this process it is important to apply various checks at different intervals to ascertain adequate progress is being maintained in the achievement of the goals. "Those most likely to succeed in life" and with this process "believe they can exert some measure of control over their own destiny. Steiner p. 311. When you believe you can change, then you are already ahead of the game.

Using a strategic action plan to map out your future helps to organize your change effort. "In man, learning seems to depend on organization. Where organization is naturally strong, association occurs spontaneously". Kottler p. 275. What this method does is force us to have an organized system of goal achievement and therefore allows many opportunities to provide positive recognition for goal achievement. When constructing the action plan each goal should have immediate, short term, and long term objectives. This allows for a step by step program of goal attainment and step by step opportunities for recognition. In concluding this book I would like to leave you with this quote from a very famous author who is responsible for many people who has achieved remarkable success using his principles. Napoleon Hill in his book Think and Grow Rich gave us this statement:

"Whatever

The Mind of Man

Can

Conceive

And

Believe

It can

Achieve"

Mission Statement

VALUES

Goals

SPIRITUAL GOALS

Education Goals

Recreation Goals

Finance Goals

HEALTH GOALS

Strategic Action Plan

Strategic Action Plan

Strategic Action Plan

Strategic Action Plan

Strategic Plan

References

Bland, Glenn (1972) <u>Success: The Glenn Bland Method, How to set goals and make plans that really work,</u> Tyndale House Publishers, Inc, Wheaton, Illinois

Carpenter, Finley (1974) <u>The Skinner Primer Behind Freedom and</u>

<u>Dignity,</u> The Free Press

Costall, Alan and Arthur Still (1987) <u>Cognitive Psychology in Question,</u> St. Martins Press, New York, N.Y.

Covey, Stephen R. (1990) <u>The 7 habits of Highly Effective People</u> Fireside, New York, N.Y.

Dudycha, George J. (1963) Applied Psychology, The Ronald Press Company, New York

Ferster, C. B., Stuart Culbertson, and Mary Carol Perrott Boren (1975)

2nd Edition Behavior Principles, Prentice Hall Inc., Englewood Cliffs, N. J.

Gallagher, J. Roswell, M. D. and Herbert I. Harris M. D. (1958)

Emotional Problems of Adolescents, Oxford University Press, New York

Heisler, Florence (1955) An Elementary School Background For Vocational Guidance, Elementary School Journal 55, 513-516 [100] Hill, Napoleon (1960)

Think and Grow Rich Combined Registry Company,   Charleston, South Carolina

Horney, Karen M. D. (1942) Self Analysis, W. W. Norton & Company New York

Kiev, Ari (1973) A Strategy for Daily Living, The Free Press, New York

Kottler, Dr. Wolfgang (1970) Gestalt Psychology, Live Right Publishing New York, N.Y.

Land, Joe, <u>The Power of Change</u> Volume One

Preble, Robert C. (1958) <u>Britannica World Language Dictionary,</u> Funk and Wagnalls Company, New York, N.Y.

Robbins, Anthony, (1986) <u>Unlimited Power</u> Fireside, New York, NY

Sharpe, Dr. Robert and David Lewis, <u>The Success Factor</u>

Steiner, George A. (1979) <u>Strategic Planning</u> The Free Press, New York, NY

<u>The New Lexicon Webster's Dictionary of the English Language</u> (1998) Lexicon Publications Inc. New York, NY

James, William (1983) <u>The Principles of Psychology</u>, Harvard University Press Cambridge Massachusetts and London England

About the Author

Ronald K. Claiborne is a pastor, musician, teacher, writer and business owner. He graduated from the University of Phoenix with a Master's in Business Administration and St. Paul's college with a B. S. degree in Accounting.

Claiborne spends a lot of his time teaching workshops to various church groups on various topics. He is the founder and owner of King James Publication and Consulting Company LLC. His passion is helping others achieve success in their business and personal lives.

Mr. Claiborne is fifty years old and lives in Scottsburg, Virginia with his wife, children, and grandchildren.